D1244542

A History of American Music

BLUES

Christopher Handyside

Heinemann Library
Chicago, Illinois

Photo research by Hannah Taylor, Maria Joannou,
and Erica Newbery
Designed by Philippa Baile and Ron Kamen
Printed in China by WKT Company Limited

10 09 08 07 06
10 9 8 7 6 5 4 3 2 1

Library of Congress Cataloging-in-Publication Data
Handyside, Chris.
Blues / Christopher Handyside.
p. cm. – (A history of American music)
Includes bibliographical references (p.   ) and
index.
ISBN 1-4034-8148-2 (hc)
1. Blues (Music)–History and criticism–Juvenile
literature. I. Title.
ML3521.H35 2006
781.643'0973–dc22   2005019280

Acknowledgments
The author and publishers are grateful to the
following for permission to reproduce copyright
material:
British Museum, London pp. 8–9 (Werner Forman
Archive); Corbis pp. 10–11 (Michael Maslan Historic
Photographs), 42 (Images Distribution), 43 (Tim
Mosenfelder); Corbis/Bettman pp. 7, 15 top, 32–33,
38; Corbis/Hulton-Deutch p. 17; Getty Images pp.
20, 39 top (Blank Archives), 40 top (Evan Agostini),
4, 6, 22, 25, 30, 39 bottom (Hulton Archive); Library
of Congress pp. 12, 15 bottom; Redferns pp. 41
(David Redfern), 27 (Deltahaze Corporation),
5 (Ebet Roberts), 36 (Jeremy Fletcher), 23 (Keith
Morris), 19, 28, 29, 31, 34–35 (Michael Ochs
Archive); Rex Features pp. 37 (Everett Collection),
40 bottom (Andre Csillag).

Cover photograph of a blues musician
reproduced with permission of Redferns
(James Fraher).

The publishers would like to thank Patrick Allen for
his assistance with the preparation of this book.

Every effort has been made to contact copyright
holders of any material reproduced in this book.
Any omissions will be rectified in subsequent
printings if notice is given to the publishers.

Words shown in **boldface** are defined in the
glossary on page 46.

Contents

What is The Blues? 04

The Seeds of The Blues 06

The Early Forms of The Blues 10

Folk and Delta Blues 14

Blues Goes on The Road 16

Early Blues Recordings 20

City Blues Roots 24

Folk Blues in The 1930s 26

The Birth of Modern Blues in Chicago 28

Jump Blues 32

Blues in Britain 36

Blues in The 1950s and 1960s' Folk Revival 38

Rock 'n' Roll and The Blues 40

The Blues Lives On 42

Timeline 44

Glossary 46

Further Information 47

Index 48

What is The Blues?

The blues began as means of expression for rural African Americans living in the South. Like jazz and rock 'n' roll, the word "blues" describes not just the music, but also the mood of the performer. In this respect, the blues has always been the music of hard times.

Blues began as rural folk music. Later, in the 1920s, it was used as the basis for the exciting sounds of jazz. Blues was plugged in and amplified when many black performers moved to northern industrial cities to find work. When rock 'n' roll was born in the 1950s, it took inspiration from the blues. In the 1960s, African Americans were fighting for civil rights. The direct language of folk blues songs spoke to them. When blues music reached the shores of England in the 1960s, artists such as the Rolling Stones and Led Zeppelin turned it into a new form.

Perhaps because of its simplicity and directness, blues has survived and evolved with the changes in culture in the United States over more than 100 years.

Muddy Waters was one of the most important and influential blues musicians of the twentieth century.

The modern sound of White Stripes' singer, songwriter, and guitarist Jack White is grounded in a love of blues and American folk music.

The Seeds of The Blues

Although the blues is a uniquely American form of music, its origins lie in African slavery. In 1619, the first ship loaded with slaves left Africa to cross the Middle Passage of the Atlantic Ocean. The ship was headed for the English Colonies that would eventually become the United States. These Africans came from different tribes and spoke different languages. They all carried with them different religious, musical, historical, and storytelling traditions.

When the Africans were sold into slavery, they were split up from other tribe members and often from their own families. This was done on purpose, because the owners didn't want their slaves to be able to talk and plan rebellion. Most of these slaves ended up on plantations, working in the fields with other Africans. They often had trouble communicating with one another. So, the slaves developed **work songs** and **field hollers** as a common language and to ease the boredom of the manual labor. This is really where the blues was born.

The children of African-American slaves were forced to work long hours in the field alongside their parents.

These work songs and field hollers, used what was called the **call-and-response form**. One singer would deliver a lyric with the song's melody and a simple phrase, or the "call." Then other singers, usually whoever was in listening distance, would sing a "response". In this way, slaves were able to communicate while they worked. They could talk about ordinary things, like the arrival of their master or the end of a day's work. They also shared important information, like plans for an after-hours religious ceremony. These hollers also allowed slaves to share the songs that they remembered from their African homeland. The call-and-response form helped to preserve the native culture of the earliest African Americans.

*Messages and stories in field hollers were part of the largely **oral tradition** of American folk and blues music, passed through person to person down the generations.*

Instruments of the blues

Many of the instruments blues players used were also of African origin. West Africa was home to a type of flute that became a key instrument in the "fife and drums" blues music that developed in the hills of northern Mississippi. Flutes were sometimes made from cane stems by African-American slaves. West Africa was also home to the drum, which was the foundation of all rhythm. In many southern states, slaves were banned from using drums in case they "drummed up" rebellion. The banjo was also an instrument of African origin that influenced the way blues artists played the guitar.

Perhaps the most unique instrument was the diddley-bow. This was a single piece of string stretched tightly between two posts. It was usually attached to a board or sometimes even onto the side of a house. Like a one-string guitar, the diddley-bow could be plucked, or it could be used as a percussion instrument by sliding a stick or bottle along the string. This made a weepy sound that would become the foundation of the slide guitar style of blues playing.

Drums are a key instrument in West African musical culture. African-American slaves brought their musical knowledge and skills from Africa to their new environment in the southern states of America.

The Early Forms of The Blues

What we now know as the blues began to develop after slavery was outlawed in 1865. In the early 1900s, African Americans found it difficult to find jobs. This was made worse in the South because of the racist **Jim Crow laws**, a segregated and unequal school system, and other factors. In the Mississippi Delta, the black population outnumbered the white population four to one. Life was especially bad for black people there. Mob **lynchings** of African Americans became more and more frequent.

Even though they had been freed from slavery, African Americans who lived in southern rural areas still found themselves living and working in terrible conditions. There were very few outlets for individual creativity and expression. The problems that African Americans faced living in the South were the real source of the blues. No one can say for sure what the first blues song was, but it was around this time in the early 1900s that people started referring to the songs of hardship, sung by rural African Americans, as the blues.

The living conditions for most African Americans in the South were extremely harsh in the early 1900s.

The earlier call-and-response style recalling the days of field hollers could be heard in the blues' repetitive verses. However, as the blues developed in its early years, it incorporated the storytelling style of the folk ballads sung by rural whites of mainly English and Scottish descent. African legends and uniquely American tall tales, such as the tale of John Henry, were set to the blues' heavy, strummed acoustic guitar.

The blues also featured a specific kind of singing to represent hard work and loneliness—with moans, hums, and whistles. Songs made up of these various noises were created on the spot. This loose spirit of **improvisation** had an influence on the development of **jazz** when the blues moved to the big cities.

*The bluesmen of the early 1900s often played on homemade instruments, like the one on the right. Both players have **kazoos** in their mouths.*

What makes a blues song?

Most blues songs follow the same layout or "chord progression." A bar is a measure of length in a song, and in the case of the blues each line of a song's verse is made up of four bars. There are three bars per verse. The basic structure of a blues song is called a "12-bar."

The rhyming of blues lyrics is predictable, too. The first two lines repeat, and the third line comments on the rhyme in the first two lines. In poetic terms, this is referred to as an **AAB rhyme scheme**.

This illustration of guitar sheet music (below) shows the basic 12-bar blues pattern. Each letter represents a chord. Three chords make up the pattern. In a blues song, these chords are repeated again and again.

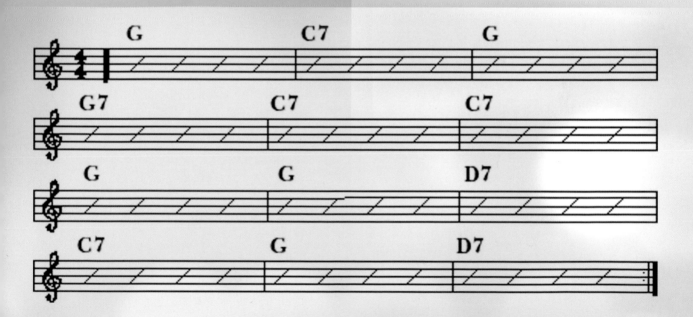

Folk and Delta Blues

From 1900 to about 1920, the blues developed differently in different areas of the South. From North Carolina to Texas, and every region in between, the blues from each area had a slightly different sound. Most blues performers were learning their songs from one another. This form of the blues, based on oral tradition, is referred to as "folk blues." Often the singers of these early songs would tell boastful stories about themselves, or sing songs that were unique to their area.

Some performers became popular enough in their local community that they were able to play their music for audiences in other towns. Others simply decided to travel, playing in towns for tips and trying to make names for themselves. In this way, the songs and styles of the blues spread and the influence of one region could be heard in the music of another. The more up-tempo style of Texas artists met with the slow, deliberate style of the Mississippi Delta.

Due to the influence and powerful performances of such artists as Charlie Patton, the Delta blues became the best-known form of the blues. Patton played his guitar like it was also a drum and put on wild, acrobatic live shows. His on-stage movements were almost gymnastic. Patton also had students that included slide guitar innovator Son House and the powerhouse shouter Howlin' Wolf. These two artists' style and popularity greatly influenced the course of the blues. Wolf's music even affected rock 'n' roll.

However, regional differences never really died out. Even within Mississippi, the style of the blues in the northern hill country was different than in other areas of the state. This style was a typical mix of African and European musical traditions. It was characterized by its use of the fife, a flute-like instrument, and marching-band type drums. Where other blues consisted of largely solo performances, this blues was a group effort that employed **syncopation**. In fact, because the northern hill country of Mississippi was so isolated, this kind of blues stayed quite close to the African music that the slaves, and later free African Americans, played in this region. With the mass production of phonograph recordings of blues artists, this era of folk blues and oral tradition came to a close in the early 1920s.

W.C. Handy is known as the "father of the blues." Considering the wide and varied roots of the blues, it is nearly impossible to pin the title on one man. Handy wasn't the first to play the blues. However, in the early 1900s, he was the first widely popular bandleader to figure out that folk blues would be a means to sell tickets to his band's shows.

In 1912, Handy became the first artist to publish a song with the word "blues" in the title. The sheet music for "Memphis Blues" was a hit, but his second blues song, "St. Louis Blues," remains one of the most popular songs of the last 100 years.

W.C. Handy helped the blues to cross over to a mainstream audience.

Blues Goes on The Road

In the 1920s, traveling medicine shows were a form of entertainment and sales. Salesmen would try to get people in rural areas to buy suspect "cure-alls" and other weird medicines. These shows often employed blues musicians as a way to gather a crowd. This spread the blues throughout the rural South and as far west as Texas, where artists such as Blind Lemon Jefferson were already well known. The first male blues recording was made in 1926 by Blind Lemon Jefferson. He went on to record more than 100 songs in less than three years. His recordings were so successful in the South that record labels in New York City and Chicago sent representatives to the South to look for new talent.

In the mid-1920s, **talent scouts**, such as Ralph Peer, were sent on the road with portable recording equipment to record for major labels, like Victor and Columbia. Their assignment was to uncover new talent. The new recording technology also made it possible for **archivists** such as John Lomax, and later his son Alan, to record folk and blues music in its native environment.

These archival recordings were made to ensure that the songs and the culture that produced them were documented and remembered. The elder Lomax made one of the most important musical "discoveries" in the development and popularity of both blues and folk music. While recording songs at Louisiana State Penitentiary for the Library of Congress in 1933, he met Huddie "Leadbelly" Ledbetter.

A circuit developed for the live performance of blues throughout the South and Midwest. Chicago and Detroit were favorite destinations for blues musicians starting in the 1920s. This was because of the abundance of jobs at new factories. Artists could either find an audience for their music, or jobs to help tide them over until they hit the road again. A thriving blues scene also developed in Indianapolis, Indiana, thanks to its central geographic location.

Memphis Tennessee in the 1920s.

Memphis, Tennessee was another hot spot on the southern live blues circuit, due to its central position in the southern railroads and main automobile routes. Artists could drive, hitchhike, or hop trains to Memphis and find a gig at any number of clubs along the city's main nightlife drag, Beale Street. It was a true crossroads.

Leadbelly

Huddie "Leadbelly" Ledbetter made, arguably, a bigger impact on both early blues and folk music than any other artist. Born in 1885, in Mooringsport, Louisiana, Leadbelly came from a musical family. He learned how to play guitar from his uncles, and he learned to play the blues at the feet of Blind Lemon Jefferson. In 1918, Leadbelly was sentenced to prison for murder. He was released in 1925, and spent several years playing and performing music while paying his rent with whatever jobs came his way. But in 1930, Leadbelly went to prison again, this time for attempted murder. While serving time, he was "discovered" by Library of Congress archivist John Lomax, on one of his journeys through the South. The Louisiana prison was a work camp, and Leadbelly led prison work songs.

Lomax recorded Leadbelly leading work chants, as well as his solo songs on the acoustic guitar. When Leadbelly was released from prison in 1934, Lomax employed Leadbelly as his driver and guide throughout the South. The pair searched out and recorded folk-blues talent in prisons and in remote country corners that Lomax alone would never have found. Leadbelly released his first record in 1935 for the American Record Company (ARC). At the time of his death in 1949, he had recorded hundreds of songs for several record labels. He remained an artist who only played music he had learned in the rural South and helped folklorists to document many songs that otherwise would have been lost forever. He also bridged the gap between the old world of acoustic, country, rural folk and blues, and the popular electric blues music of the city.

Leadbelly is still considered one of America's greatest musical treasures.

19

Early Blues Recordings

Though records and record players became available in the early 1900s, they were a luxury that most rural African Americans could not afford. But with the beginning of mass-produced recordings, the blues successfully made the transition from folk to popular music.

Mamie Smith typically sang about bluesy topics, like heartbreak, frustration, and revenge.

Officially, the first blues song on record was "Crazy Blues," recorded by Mamie Smith and The Jazz Hounds for Okeh Records in August of 1920. The record was a hit, and it made Smith a star.

This ushered in an era in which both black blues artists and white pop artists often recorded the same song—one for black audiences and one for white audiences. The largest record labels found that white record stores would not carry blues records made by blacks. However, they had no problem selling the bluesy records to black audiences. These blues records by black artists were referred to as "race records." From the 1920s to the early 1950s, blues recordings were almost always recorded for African Americans. However, many of these records still managed to cross over to a mainstream, white audience.

When the **Great Depression** hit in 1929, most people could no longer afford to buy records. Many record companies went out of business and only the biggest labels survived. However, blues musicians continued to play to live audiences, and record—mostly at studios in Chicago, which was home to some major talent scouts.

More people flocked to Chicago when the production boom for World War II began, and many good factory jobs became available. Many of the South's biggest blues names either moved to Chicago permanently or spent significant time there. The city became the home of the blues and the center for record companies interested in recording blues music. Chicago also had a thriving jazz scene on "the stroll"—a stretch of Michigan Avenue and State Street that was densely packed with dozens of clubs.

One popular artist who moved from Birmingham, Alabama to Chicago was Clarence "Pinetop" Smith. Smith played "boogie-woogie" piano. Boogie-woogie is an upbeat style of piano playing. A chugging rhythm is played on the left hand and a frantic, often improvised, melody with the right hand. It was well suited to the rowdy house parties where blues musicians played when no nightclub gigs were available. It also made people want to dance. Smith's "Pine Top's Boogie-Woogie" was a hit record and influenced a generation of both blues and jazz piano players.

Bessie Smith played a key role in popularizing the blues in the 1920s.

Women sing the blues

Janis Joplin admired and respected Bessie Smith so much that she eventually paid for Bessie's gravestone.

When the blues was first recorded, women proved to be the most popular attractions on record. This was strange because in its folk blues years, before blues was recorded, it was dominated by men. So when Mamie Smith, Bessie Smith, and Sippie Wallace became stars, it was unexpected. Women gave the female point of view to the blues stories of heartbreak and woe. Female blues singers were also more attractive to audiences. While male blues performers were content to dust off their coats and maybe put on a tie, female singers got dressed up in style. With their brassy singing style, they easily won over the crowds during the 1920s and 1930s.

During this period, jazz musicians were putting on glitzy performances with big bands. The female blues acts seemed to fit in well with this scene. Bessie Smith's expressive and boisterous style set the tone for the confident, powerful female blues singers (or "shouters" as they were sometimes called) that followed her. Sippie Wallace, Etta James, and Koko Taylor, in the 1940s, 1950s, and 1960s, carried on the tradition of the female blues shouter. In the late 1960s, Texan singer Janis Joplin brought the gritty power and passion of the early blues singers to the Woodstock generation of rock 'n' rollers. In the 1970s, slide guitarist Bonnie Raitt carried on the tradition, adding her smooth-but-smoky vocals to her **virtuoso** guitar playing. Today, Bessie Smith's influence can be heard in the music of artists as diverse as rocker Melissa Etheridge and pop-soul singer Joss Stone.

City Blues Roots

Despite the hard economic times, a blossoming music industry in Chicago meant steady work for southern blues musicians who had moved north. Chicago offered state-of-the-art recording studios. Blues musicians could record their music with the hopes of becoming rich and famous, or at least well known and able to pay the bills.

Because of the lingering effects of the Great Depression, many people still couldn't afford to buy records, let alone the record players to play them. So in the mid 1930s, jukeboxes were put into bars. For the odd dime, people could select a handful of tunes and enjoy them in the company of their friends. This was the way that many blues musicians got their music heard. Jukeboxes became extremely popular. Bars that had jukeboxes became known as "juke joints." They were places where African Americans could get together after work and dance to the latest records.

The jukebox audience always wanted new songs, so more southern blues men and women were able to make records. At first, these were **acoustic** records, featuring guitar, piano, bass, and occasionally the harmonica. But eventually acoustic folk-blues styles gave way to amplified electric guitar.

By the end of the 1930s, many of the top blues guitarists, like Big Bill Broonzy and Lonnie Johnson, were recording with electric guitars. Over the next 15 years, this electric-guitar based blues would come to be the signature sound of Chicago musicians.

Big Bill Broonzy was one of the first blues guitarists to switch to electric amplification.

Folk Blues in the 1930s

While the blues was finding its city sound in Chicago in the 1930s, folk blues was still going strong in the South. In fact, two of the blues' most revered artists were just starting their careers. The first generation of recorded blues artists such as Charley Patton, Son House, and Blind Lemon Jefferson had passed along their tricks of the trade to a younger bunch of players. These men would become **icons** of the blues in the next twenty years.

First among these icons was Robert Johnson, born in 1911 in Hazlehurst, Mississippi. Son House was a major influence on Johnson when he was learning to play the blues. In his early years, Johnson would often try to sit in with House and other well-known Delta blues players. By the mid-1930s, Johnson had mastered the guitar and was ready to conquer the blues world. But he had a short-lived career. In fact, he had only a handful of recording sessions in the years 1936 and 1937. The majority of these took place in hotels while he was on the road.

Johnson constantly played shows as though he was on borrowed time. Perhaps because of this sense of urgency, the powerful force of his emotional and haunted performances had an impact on blues playing and blues mythology for generations to come. Among the songs that Johnson wrote and recorded that have become blues standards are "Cross Road Blues," "Stop Breakin' Down Blues," and "Hell Hound on My Trail."

When Johnson died in 1938, aged 27, his songs became the stuff of legends. His few recordings were powerful enough for him to be crowned king of the blues when his songs were **anthologized** in the 1961 album *Robert Johnson: King of the Delta Blues Singers*.

Singer and guitarist Robert Johnson is as well known for his legend as he is for his music.

"The Crossroads"

The legend goes that, in 1936, Robert Johnson made a deal with the Devil to gain immortal fame as a musician. One night, Johnson supposedly traveled to "the Crossroads"—a spot where two roads crossed near a plantation in Dockery, Mississippi. Crossroads figure prominently in blues mythology and, **Voudon** (or Voodoo). At midnight, the Devil appeared to Johnson and the deal was made. The Devil tuned Johnson's guitar. In exchange for his mortal soul, Johnson would gain everlasting fame as a blues guitarist and singer.

Afterward, Johnson was constantly haunted by feverish dreams and visions. He saw the Devil in the form of a hellhound chasing his every move. Johnson went on to become famous with songs such as "Hell Hound on My Trail," "Me and the Devil Blues," and "Cross Road Blues." He made dozens of recordings in the brief period between 1936 and 1937, and traveled nonstop throughout the South and Midwest. Then, one night in August 1938, someone poisoned his jug of whiskey. Ironically, Johnson recovered from the poisoning, but died three days later from pneumonia that he caught while he was recuperating. Though only two known photographs and a handful of recordings survived, Johnson's fame and legend spread. He became an important part of blues' mythology.

The Birth of Modern Blues in Chicago

In 1941, Alan Lomax was on one of his regular treks around the Deep South, when he came upon a powerhouse guitarist and tractor driver who called himself Muddy Waters. McKinley "Muddy Waters" Morganfield was born in 1915 and loved the early Delta blues sound. By the age of 17, he was a guitar **prodigy** and not afraid to boast about it. In his 1955 song "Mannish Boy," Waters claimed his mother was told that he'd be the "greatest man alive." Arrogant to be sure, but Waters' superb playing backed his boasting.

In the early 1940s, Waters moved to Chicago to record songs for a number of labels. He hit Chicago's booming blues scene just as it became electrified. Waters was now part of the Chicago scene that was filling jukeboxes with hits. However, he was playing mostly as a **session musician** on other artists' records. Then, in 1947, Leonard Chess of Chess Records noticed his playing on Sunnyland Slim's records. Chess gave Waters the chance to record his own music. Amongst Waters' first solo recordings were "I Can't Be Satisfied," a country blues tune gone electric, and "Rollin' Stone." These songs set the tone for what would become Chicago Blues. The title of one of Waters' songs later inspired the name chosen by a group of English teenagers who became one of the most popular bands in rock 'n' roll.

Muddy Waters (left) and friends in the 1940s.

After World War II, the U.S. economy was booming. Factories in cities such as Chicago, Detroit, and Indianapolis were employing a steady stream of African Americans from the South. The period from around the mid-1940s to the early 1950s was a golden age for the blues. Records coming out of Chicago were selling extremely well and blues had replaced jazz as the favorite dance music for both black and white Americans.

In 1943, another Mississippian named John Lee Hooker moved to Detroit, Michigan to get work in one of the Ford factories. He soon discovered that Detroit's Hastings Street was a fertile ground for blues gigs. Hooker also discovered that amplified electric guitar presented a whole new world of opportunities. He made up songs in his head while working on the line for Ford Motor Company. In 1948, he recorded "Boogie Chillen'" which became a big hit on the blues scene. During the 1940s and 1950s, Hooker went on to record and perform a string of songs, including "Boom Boom" and "Dimples."

John Lee Hooker's music put Detroit on the blues map.

Jump Blues

When they weren't making blues records for jukeboxes or working day jobs, blues musicians were often trading musical ideas with Chicago's many jazz musicians. The blues may have been looked upon as the less sophisticated of the two styles, but musicians from both the jazz and the blues world influenced each other.

An example of this in the late 1940s and the early 1950s was the rise in popularity of a style called "**jump blues**." Sometimes called "jump jazz," the jump blues of the 1940s often followed the AAB rhyme scheme of the blues.

Jump blues made people want to dance! The bands often included the horns—saxophone, cornet, and trombone—that had become common in jazz. It was a potent mixture that greatly influenced another American music genre, rhythm and blues (R&B). R&B was originally an up-tempo version of the blues, played by a smaller band, that got people in bars and taverns dancing. The blues sang about hard times, but jump blues had a more upbeat approach to life. Essentially, jump blues was all about having a good time!

Jump blues was the most popular sound around in the early 1950s.

While blues was heard most often in juke joints on jukeboxes, jump blues was a live event. The so-called "jazz age" of the 1920s had already helped get people used to jazz sounds. Now the "big band" era of jazz took hold with music played by large jazz combos, such as Louis Jordan, Benny Goodman, and Tommy Dorsey.

In the dancehalls of cities like Chicago, Memphis, and New York City, this mix of jazz and blues created a powerful musical force. As the 1940s came to a close, the instrumentation, spirit, and songs of jump blues began to influence the music that would be called rock 'n' roll. In fact, the music of the first generation of rockers, especially Chuck Berry, was often just a simplified, stripped-down, and amplified version of the jump blues music of artists such as Louis Jordan.

By the 1950s, as jump blues was being taken up by rock 'n' rollers, the blues was injecting jump blues with its style once again. The result was rhythm and blues, or R&B. In one form or another, R&B became the dominant strain of black music for the next five decades.

Louis Jordan's band music made the blues jump! He continued to release popular records into the 1950s.

Blues in Britain

In the 1950s, top American blues musicians traveled to Britain and Europe, winning rave reviews and gaining international fans. At that time it was still difficult for black blues artists to perform in white nightclubs in the United States. The only white audiences many black blues musicians played for were in the United Kingdom and Europe. British musicians were fascinated with the blues and a devoted pool of fans devoured any American blues record they could get their hands on. In the early 1960s, Willie Dixon, Howlin' Wolf, Muddy Waters, Delta-blues harmonica virtuoso Sonny Boy Williamson, and other prominent blues musicians went to Europe for a festival called the American Folk Blues Festival. The Festival ran for ten more years, cementing the reputation of American blues artists in Europe.

In London's fashionable music scene, Alexis Korner was a genuine blues enthusiast. There were no blues' clubs in London in 1962, so Korner and his bandmate Cyril Davies opened one. Three young music enthusiasts—Mick Jagger, Keith Richards, and Brian Jones—were impressed with Korner's joint. They quickly formed a band with Korner's friend Charlie Watts and Bill Wyman. Two years later that band, the Rolling Stones, recorded a song at Chess Studios called "2120 S. Michigan," paying their respects to artists Muddy Waters and Howlin' Wolf.

The Rolling Stones' sound never wandered too far from the blues.

Korner's club soon became a "swinging London" hotspot and was also visited by a young guitarist named Jimmy Page and his pal, Eric Clapton. The two went on to form a blues/rock 'n' roll band, the Yardbirds. Page then left the Yardbirds to form the band Led Zeppelin in 1968. Led Zeppelin became hugely successful worldwide with their blend of hard rock and the blues. In 1985, the band was successfully sued by Chess Records because of the similarities between Zeppelin's song "Whole Lotta Love" and Muddy Waters' version of Dixon's song "You Need Love." The effect of this was to give the blues more publicity.

In the early 1970s, Led Zeppelin became one of the most popular bands in the world.

Clapton went on to form a blues-based hard rock trio, Cream. Clapton also had a successful solo career that included the 2004 release of his Grammy-nominated tribute to Robert Johnson, *Me and Mr. Johnson*.

Surprisingly, one of the most legendary musicians to become famous in London was from Seattle, Washington. James (Jimi) Marshall Hendrix landed in England, in 1967. In 1966, a member of a British band, The Animals, had seen Hendrix play in a small club in New York. He convinced Hendrix to pack up and move to London. Hendrix's guitar playing mixed the emerging experimentation of rock 'n' roll with his roots in R&B. With his wild stage presence, Hendrix became immediately popular in London's rock scene. When he played one concert in 1967, members of the Beatles were seated right up front. To their amazement, Hendrix played their latest track, "Sgt. Pepper's Lonely Hearts Club Band," right through, having only heard it once earlier that day.

Blues in The 1950s and 1960s' Folk Revival

As the blues was finding new popularity overseas, the music's pioneers were finally gaining new attention back home. In 1952, a record collector and filmmaker named Harry Smith released a three-volume collection called *The Anthology of American Folk Music*. The *Anthology* was actually a collection of mostly long-forgotten recordings from the 1920s and 1930s. It featured such blues artists as Blind Lemon Jefferson and Mississippi John Hurt, along with very early recordings of country artists. The collection caught the attention of folk artists, such as Pete Seeger and Bob Dylan, as well as a new generation of musicians playing rock 'n' roll and folk music.

Then in 1959, the renowned folklorist Alan Lomax released a collection called *Blues in the Mississippi Night*, an album of recordings he had made while traveling through the South in 1946. It included songs by previously unknown folk-blues artists such as Big Bill Broonzy, Sonny Boy Williamson, and many others.

Young musicians interested in the roots of folk and the blues now had a lot of great music to dig through. The anthologies became the foundation of the so-called "folk revival" of the 1950s and 1960s. These were the musicians that later became known as the "Woodstock Generation," among them Bob Dylan, the Grateful Dead, Janis Joplin, the Byrds, and Creedence Clearwater Revival.

The Grateful Dead in the mid-1960s.

The Newport Folk Festival was where many of the new fans of this old American music first saw artists such as Son House and others. Created in 1959, the Rhode Island festival was the gathering place for thousands of fans who had become fascinated by the roots music of the United States. Newport, and other major folk festivals in cities like Berkley and Chicago in the early 1960s through the mid-1970s, put the aging, early blues artists back on the map and allowed them to pursue music full-time.

More importantly, the rediscovery of these artists introduced the music of the rural South to the **civil rights movement**—the cultural and political effort to attain equal rights for African Americans that took place during the 1950s and 1960s. The impact was felt through specific songs, especially the post-slavery spirituals that were often sung to inspire protests. In this way, the blues helped to develop a growing cultural awareness of African-American history.

Son House's solo performance style was unique.

Another fan of country blues was businessman and promoter Dick Waterman. Waterman helped relaunch the careers of many early blues artists during this period. But a simple phone call from Waterman in Mississippi to Rochester, New York, one day in 1964, led to Waterman's greatest "discovery."

The influential Delta Blues pioneer, Son House, was living in Rochester at the time. House's style of slide guitar had influenced a generation of guitar players in the 1930s. He often sang his songs of heartache and redemption in a husky, baritone **a capella**, stomping out the rhythm with his feet. Thanks to Waterman's phone call, House enjoyed a successful second career that lasted for twenty years. He died in Detroit in 1988.

Son House's real age had never been determined, but on several occasions he said that he was born in 1886. He would have been age 102 when he died, playing music well into his 90s!

Rock 'n' Roll and The Blues

By the 1970s and 1980s, a second and third generation of musicians raised on rock were mixing their love of the blues with the volume, instrumentation, and attitude of rock 'n' roll. By this time, the blues was no longer a mainly African-American style. More white performers were playing the blues in bars across the country, taking their inspiration from rock 'n' roll and the Chicago Blues sound.

Bonnie Raitt's style mixes folk blues and rock-based electric sounds.

ZZ Top are known for their trademark long beards and loud blues-based guitar playing.

In 1967, Dick Waterman signed a young slide guitar player fresh out of Radcliffe College. Her name was Bonnie Raitt. Raitt was an avid follower of the folk-blues players and often sat in with older musicians, including Mississippi Fred McDowell and Sippie Wallace. Raitt's husky voice and passionate singing quickly became popular. However, she was only truly respected amongst other musicians and critics until her 1989's album *Nick of Time*, which sold more millions of copies and earned Raitt her first Grammy. She continues to record and recently participated in the 2005 Grammy-winning album *Genius Loves Company*, featuring the late R&B pioneer Ray Charles.

Further blurring the lines between hard rock and the blues was ZZ Top. The band's more bluesy 1970s sound, such as their 1973 hit "La Grange" (based on John Lee Hooker's "Boogie Chillen'") gave way in the 1980s to pop-based hits, such as "Sharp-Dressed Man."

The 1980 movie *The Blues Brothers* also helped to put the Chicago Blues sound on the map. Starring comedians John Belushi and Dan Ackroyd, the film also featured Memphis R&B musicians Matt "Guitar" Murphy and Donald "Duck" Dunne, John Lee Hooker, plus R&B stars Ray Charles, James Brown, and Aretha Franklin. Because it was based in Chicago and featured two very popular white comedians acting like seasoned blues performers, *The Blues Brothers* helped the blues style to become even more popular to a growing, largely white audience.

Buddy Guy was another Chicago guitar player who really caught onto Chicago's searing electric blues sound in the late 1950s. Following in the footsteps of his idol, Muddy Waters, Guy recorded a string of records for Chess in the 1960s. But it was his energetic live performances that really made him a popular blues star in the 1970s. In 1989, he opened Buddy Guy's Legends in Chicago's South Loop area, where he and visiting blues legends, such as Eric Clapton and many others, came to play. The club remains a must-visit destination to many fans of the blues across the country.

Guy was a major influence on the artist who pushed blues-rock's popularity furthest. In the 1980s, Dallas guitar virtuoso Stevie Ray Vaughan and his band Double Trouble pulled their sound from rock, blues, and jazz. They soon caught the attention of a large following of critics, fans, and other musicians. In 1983, Double Trouble released its debut album, *Texas Flood*. It was the first of a string of records that sold more than 500,000 copies. By the spring of 1990, Vaughan was a star. He had just recorded an album with his brother Jimmie when his plane crashed after a gig in Wisconsin, killing all on board.

Stevie Ray Vaughan is considered one of the most influential electric blues players in history.

The Blues Lives On

The enduring spirit of the blues and its musical flexibility lives on. More than 100 years since its birth, blues is still being played in both country (acoustic) and city (electric) forms.

Hotshot guitarists, such as Jonny Lang, have continued in the newer tradition of electric blues players like Buddy Guy, Robert Cray, and Stevie Ray Vaughan. Even the Rolling Stones, and Boston-based arena rock stars Aerosmith have returned to blues roots, releasing albums of **covers** and pre-rock blues. Thanks to the ongoing efforts of Mississippi-based blues label, Fat Possum, there has also been renewed interest in blues artists from the South, such as R. L. Burnside, Junior Kimbrough, and others,

Steven Tyler and guitarist Joe Perry of Aerosmith performing in 2004.

In 1997, Harry Smith's *The Anthology of American Folk Music* was rereleased on CD. Just two years later, in 1999, Alan Lomax's original field recordings of blues artists also made a real impact. On his 1999 album, *Play*, electronic artist Moby used Lomax's recordings as **samples** and the foundation for his mix of dance beats and very modern arrangements. This powerful combination was nominated for a Grammy Award in 2000. More importantly, it reignited an interest in folk blues among listeners of popular music.

However, that short burst of interest in the blues was nothing compared to what was to come. In 2003, a couple of young Detroit musicians, The White Stripes, released their fourth album, *Elephant*. It soon gained multi-platinum sales. Again, the album was a combination of primal rock 'n' roll and country blues. The White Stripes regularly included songs by Leadbelly, Son House, Charlie Patton, and Robert Johnson in their live shows. As much as the blues has changed over the years, the spirit of the music remains the same.

Much of The White Stripes' sound is based in their love of American folk-blues music.

Timeline

1619 The first slave ship crosses the Middle Passage of the Atlantic Ocean. African music was brought to North America. This would become the backbone for blues, jazz, country, R&B, and rock.

1861–1865 American Civil War. This war between the Union and the Confederacy ended in 1865 with the defeat of the Confederates.

1865 Thirteenth Amendment to the U.S. Constitution abolishes slavery.

1877 Invention of the phonograph by Thomas Edison.

1885 Huddie "Leadbelly" Ledbetter is born.

1911 Robert Johnson is born.

1912 W.C. Handy issues "Memphis Blues," the first published blues song.

1914–1918 World War I. This war was fought between France, Britain, and the United States against Germany. Germany was defeated in 1918. The United States did not enter the war until 1917.

1920 Mamie Smith records "Crazy Blues."

1920 Commercial radio broadcasting begins in the United States.

1920–1929 The "Roaring Twenties." This decade is also known as the "Jazz Age."

1926 Blind Lemon Jefferson records the first blues song to be sung by a male.

1929 The U.S. stock market crash begins the period of the 1930s known as the Great Depression.

1933 John and Alan Lomax record Leadbelly.

1935 Leadbelly releases his first record.

1938 Robert Johnson dies.

1941 The United States enters World War II. The war ends in 1945.

1947 Chess Records founded in Chicago by brothers Phil and Leonard Chess.

1948 John Lee Hooker records "Boogie Chillen'."
Muddy Waters releases debut recording "I Can't Be Satisfied" on Chess records.
Late 1940s–1973 period of U.S. involvement in Vietnam. Involvement in Vietnam in the 1960s through 1973 is commonly called the Vietnam War.

1952 Harry Smith releases *The Anthology ot American Folk Music*.

1959 The first Newport Folk Festival.
Folklorist Alan Lomax releases *Blues in the Mississippi Night*.

1963 Assassination of President John F. Kennedy on November 22nd.

1964 Civil Rights Act is signed by President Lyndon B. Johnson.

1968 Assassination of African-American Civil Rights leader, Martin Luther King Jr. in April.
Assassination of presidential candidate Robert F. Kennedy, brother of late President John F. Kennedy in June.

1969 The Woodstock Festival takes place in Bethel, N.Y..

1980 *The Blues Brothers* movie is released.

1989 Buddy Guy opens Buddy Guy's Legends nightclub in Chicago.

Glossary

a capella singing performed without the accompaniment of musical instruments

AAB rhyme scheme order of a three-line lyric in which the last syllable of the first two lines rhyme and the third line does not

acoustic instrument that does not have electric amplification

anthologize to collect the works of artists in a single presentation or record

archivist someone who seeks out, organizes, and catalogs the past work of artists

call-and-response form when the leader of a group and the chorus or other members of the group alternate performing parts of a song

civil rights movement cultural and political effort to gain equal rights for African Americans in the United States

cover when artists record their own, newer version of another artist's music

field hollers songs sung on the plantations by African-American slaves

Great Depression period from 1929 until the beginning of World War II in which the United States' economy was "depressed," or in poor shape, and many Americans were without work

house band band employed full-time by a club or record company to play with featured singers or other performers

icons those who have reached a status of adoration or high esteem

improvisation the act of composing and performing, in this case, a piece of music, without preparation

jazz original American form of music developed in New Orleans, Louisiana at the turn of the 20th century. It emphasizes individual improvisation in group performances, as well as uptempo rhythms.

Jim Crow laws laws in place in the American South from 1877 until the 1960s designed to enforce racial segregation between whites and African Americans

jump blues amplified mixture of uptempo swing jazz and blues, common in urban areas in the 1940s

kazoo small whistle-type instrument with a vibrating membrane that changes the sound of the player's voice

lynching another word for hanging, in this case, the hanging of African Americans in the American south from the time of slavery through the 1950s

oral tradition folk method by which songs and stories are passed from generation to generation

prodigy very young, talented musician

samples small pieces of music taken from one composition and used in another, as in hip-hop music

session musician musician who is not a permanent member of any particular band, but who is hired to play with bands on an occasional basis

syncopation short pause or displacement of the beat for dynamic effect

talent scouts employed by a record label or company to look for new artists

virtuoso exceptionally skilled musician or performer

Voudon (or Voodoo) religion based on African gods and the worship of dead ancestors

work songs songs sung in unison by groups of slaves and prisoners to pass the time while working

Further Information

WEBSITES

Smithsonian Music resources:

www.si.edu/resource/faq/nmah/music.htm

PLACES TO VISIT

MoMI (The Museum of Musical Instruments)

PO Box 8447

Santa Cruz, CA 95061

877-30-MUSIC

www.momi.org

An on-line "museum" with a lot of information on various instruments and genres of music.

Experience Music Project

325 5th Ave. N.

Seattle, WA 98109

877-367-5483

www.emplive.org

Huge interactive music museum and archive. Covers all types of popular music—jazz, soul/R&B, rock, country, folk, and blues.

Rock and Roll Hall of Fame Museum

One Key Plaza

751 Erieside Ave

Cleveland, OH 44114

216-781-ROCK

www.rockhall.com

Huge museum that covers rock, folk, country, R&B, blues, and jazz.

RECORDINGS

Robert Johnson:

The Best of Robert Johnson:

Traveling Riverside Blues

(Blues Forever)

Muddy Waters:

The Complete Plantation Recordings

(Chess)

Leadbelly:

The Best of Leadbelly

(Cleopatra)

Son House:

Original Delta Blues

(Sony)

Louis Jordan:

Let the Good Times Roll

(MCA)

Howlin' Wolf:

Howlin' Wolf: His Best

(Chess 50th Anniversary Collection)

John Lee Hooker:

Chill Out

(Pointblank)

Janis Joplin:

18 Essential Songs

(Sony)

The White Stripes:

Elephant

(V2)

Index

a capella singing........................ 39
acoustic blues............... 22, 24, 42
Aerosmith.................................... 42
African Americans.... 4, 10, 20, 21
                          24, 29, 39
American Folk Blues Festival... 36
Animals....................................... 37
archival recordings.................... 20

ballads.. 12
banjo... 8
Beatles.. 37
Berry, Chuck........................ 31, 34
Blues Brothers (film).......... 41, 45
blues circuit........................... 20-21
boogie-woogie............................. 21
British blues musicians...... 36-37
Broonzy, Big Bill........... 24, 25, 38
Burnside, R.L. 42
Byrds... 38

call-and-response form........... 7, 12
Charles, Ray........................... 40, 41
Chess, Leonard.............. 28, 31, 45
Chess, Phil........................... 31, 45
Chess Records.......... 28, 30, 31, 36
                          37, 41, 45
Chicago... 21, 24, 28, 29, 30, 31, 39
Chicago Blues.....24, 28, 31, 40, 41
chord progression...................... 13
civil rights movement......4, 39, 45
Clapton, Eric................... 31, 37, 41
Cray, Robert........................... 31, 42
Cream... 37
Creedence Clearwater Revival... 38

Delta blues.................... 14, 28, 39
Detroit.................................. 20, 29
Diddley, Bo................................. 31
diddley-bow................................... 8
Dixon, Willie................... 30, 31, 36
Dorsey, Tommy........................... 34
Double Trouble........................... 41
drums.................................... 8, 14
Dunne, Donald........................... 41
Dylan, Bob................................... 38

early recordings.................... 20-21
electric blues........... 18. 24, 25, 29
                          31, 41, 42
Etheridge, Melissa......................23

field hollers........................ 6, 7, 12
fife.. 14
flute.. 8
folk blues.............14, 15, 24, 26-27
                          40, 43
folk music.......... 4, 5, 7, 12, 20, 38
folk revival..........................38-39
Franklin, Aretha......................41

Goodman, Benny.........................34
Grateful Dead.............................38
Great Depression...........21, 24, 44
Guy, Buddy............. 31, 41, 42, 45

Handy, W.C. 15, 44
Hendrix, Jimi.............................. 37
Hooker, John Lee.....29, 40, 41, 45
House, Son............... 14, 26, 39, 43
Howlin' Wolf............. 14, 30, 31, 36
Hurt, Mississippi John.............. 38

improvisation..............................12
Indianapolis........................ 20, 29

Jagger, Mick................................36
James, Etta.......................... 23, 31
jazz..........4, 12, 21, 23, 29, 32, 34
Jefferson, Blind Lemon....... 20, 26
                          22, 38, 44
Jim Crow laws............................10
Johnson, Lonnie........................ 22
Johnson, Robert........13, 26-27, 37
                          43, 44, 45
Jones, Brian.................................36
Joplin, Janis........................23, 38
Jordan, Louis........................... 34
jukeboxes........................ 24, 28, 34
jump blues........................... 32, 34

kazoos... 12
Kimbrough, Junior.................... 42
King, B.B..................................... 31
Korner, Alexis............................ 36

Lang, Johnny............................. 42
Leadbelly (Huddie Ledbetter)... 20
                          22-23, 43, 44, 45
Led Zeppelin............................ 4, 37
legends and tall-tales................ 12
Little Walter........................ 30, 31
Lomax, Alan...... 20, 28, 38, 43, 44
Lomax, John................. 20, 22, 44

McDowell, Mississippi Fred....... 40
medicine shows.......................... 20
Memphis................................21, 31
Moby... 43
Murphy, Matt............................. 41
musical instruments........ 8, 12, 14
                          24, 34

Newport Folk Festival.........39, 45

oral tradition........................... 7, 14
origin of the blues...........4, 6-7, 10

Page, Jimmy............................... 37
Patton, Charlie............... 14, 26, 43
Peer, Ralph................................. 20
Perry, Joe................................... 42

race records................................ 21
Raitt, Bonnie....................... 23, 40
regional differences....................14
rhyming................................. 13, 24
rhythm & blues (R&B)...32, 34, 41
Richards, Keith........................... 36
rock 'n' roll........ 4, 14, 30, 31, 34
                          37, 38, 40-41, 43
Rogers, Jimmy...................... 30, 31
Rolling Stones...... 4, 28, 36, 37, 42
Rush, Otis................................... 31

Seeger, Pete................................ 38
session musicians....................... 28
slavery.......................6-7, 10, 44
slide guitar style.................... 8, 39
Smith, Bessie........................ 22, 23
Smith, Clarence "Pinetop"......... 21
Smith, Harry................. 38, 43, 45
Smith, Mamie......... 20, 21, 23, 44
Spann, Otis................................ 30
spirituals.................................... 39
Stone, Joss................................. 23
syncopation................................ 14

Taylor, Koko........................ 23, 31
12-bar blues pattern.................. 13
Tyler, Steven.............................. 42

Vaughan, Stevie Ray...... 31, 41, 42
Voudoun (Voodoo)...................... 27

Wallace, Sippie..................... 23, 40
Waterman, Dick.................... 39, 40
Waters, Muddy.......... 4, 28, 30, 31
                          36, 37, 41, 45
Watts, Charlie............................ 36
White, Jack.................................. 5
White Stripes.........................5, 43
Williamson, Sonny Boy........ 36, 38
women singers............................ 23
Woodstock Generation......... 23, 38
work songs.......................... 6, 7, 22
Wyman, Bill................................ 36

Yardbirds.....................................37

ZZ Top.. 40